Prince Hohenstiel-Schwangau, Saviour of Society by Robert Browning

Robert Browning is one of the most significant Victorian Poets and, of course, English Poetry.

Much of his reputation is based upon his mastery of the dramatic monologue although his talents encompassed verse plays and even a well-regarded essay on Shelley during a long and prolific career.

He was born on May 7th, 1812 in Walmouth, London. Much of his education was home based and Browning was an eclectic and studious student, learning several languages and much else across a myriad of subjects, interests and passions.

Browning's early career began promisingly. The fragment from his intended long poem Pauline brought him to the attention of Dante Gabriel Rossetti, and was followed by Paracelsus, which was praised by both William Wordsworth and Charles Dickens. In 1840 the difficult Sordello, which was seen as willfully obscure, brought his career almost to a standstill.

Despite these artistic and professional difficulties his personal life was about to become immensely fulfilling. He began a relationship with, and then married, the older and better known Elizabeth Barrett. This new foundation served to energise his writings, his life and his career.

During their time in Italy they both wrote much of their best work. With her untimely death in 1861 he returned to London and thereafter began several further major projects.

The collection Dramatis Personae (1864) and the book-length epic poem The Ring and the Book (1868-69) were published and well received; his reputation as a venerated English poet now assured.

Robert Browning died in Venice on December 12th, 1889.

Index of Contents

NOTE

Ὕδραν φονεύσας, μυρίων τ' ἄλλον πόνων
διῆλφον ἀγέλας ...
τὸ λοίσθιον δὲ τονδ' ἔτλην τάλας
πόνον,
... ~δῶμα θριγκῶσαι κακοῖς~.

I slew the Hydra, and from labor pass'd
To labor—tribes of labors! Till, at last,

Attempting one more labor, in a trice,
Alack, with ills I crowned the edifice.

This poem, written in Scotland in 1871, shortly after the downfall of Napoleon III., was published in December of the same year. The suggestion of the emperor is transparent, and Browning writing in January, 1872, to Miss Isa Blagden, says of it: "I am glad you have got my little book, and seen for yourself whether I make the best or the worst of the case. I think, in the main, he meant to do what I say, and, but for weakness—grown more apparent in his last years than formerly—would have done what I say he did not. I thought badly of him at the beginning of his career, et pour cause: better afterward, on the strength of the promises he made, and gave indications of intending to redeem. I think him very weak in the last miserable year. At his worst I prefer him to Thiers's best. I am told my little thing is succeeding—sold 1400 in the first five days, and before any notice appeared." And again, to the same correspondent: "I am glad you like what the editor of the Edinburgh calls my eulogium on the second empire—which it is not, any more than what another wiseacre affirms it to be, 'a scandalous attack on the old constant friend of England'—it is just what I imagine the man might, if he pleased, say for himself." Mrs. Browning's well-known enthusiasm for Napoleon III. as instanced in her poems unquestionably gave distinctness to Browning's own reflections. The motto is from the Hercules Furens of Euripides, vv. 1276-1280, and the translation is presumably by Browning. There is a palace Hohen-Schwangau, built by the Bavarian mad king Ludwig.

PRINCE HOHENSTIEL-SCHWANGAU, SAVIOUR OF SOCIETY

You have seen better days, dear? So have I—
And worse too, for they brought no such bud-mouth
As yours to lisp "You wish you knew me!" Well,
Wise men, 't is said, have sometimes wished the same,
And wished and had their trouble for their pains.
Suppose my Œdipus should lurk at last
Under a pork-pie hat and crinoline,
And, latish, pounce on Sphinx in Leicester Square?
Or likelier, what if Sphinx in wise old age,
Grown sick of snapping foolish people's heads,
And jealous for her riddle's proper rede,—
Jealous that the good trick which served the turn
Have justice rendered it, nor class one day
With friend Home's stilts and tongs and medium-ware,—
What if the once redoubted Sphinx, I say,
(Because night draws on, and the sands increase,
And desert-whispers grow a prophecy,)
Tell all to Corinth of her own accord,
Bright Corinth, not dull Thebes, for Laïs' sake,
Who finds me hardly gray, and likes my nose,
And thinks a man of sixty at the prime?
Good! It shall be! Revealment of myself!
But listen, for we must co-operate;
I don't drink tea: permit me the cigar!

First, how to make the matter plain, of course—
What was the law by which I lived. Let 's see:
Ay, we must take one instant of my life
Spent sitting by your side in this neat room:
Watch well the way I use it, and don't laugh!
Here 's paper on the table, pen and ink:
Give me the soiled bit—not the pretty rose!
See! having sat an hour, I 'm rested now,
Therefore want work: and spy no better work
For eye and hand and mind that guides them both,
During this instant, than to draw my pen
From blot One—thus—up, up to blot Two—thus—
Which I at last reach, thus, and here 's my line
Five inches long and tolerably straight:
Better to draw than leave undrawn, I think,
Fitter to do than let alone, I hold,
Though better, fitter, by but one degree.
Therefore it was that, rather than sit still
Simply, my right-hand drew it while my left
Pulled smooth and pinched the moustache to a point.

Now I permit your plump lips to unpurse:
"So far, one possibly may understand
Without recourse to witchcraft!" True, my dear.
Thus folks begin with Euclid,—finish, how?
Trying to square the circle!—at any rate,
Solving abstruser problems than this first,
"How find the nearest way 'twixt point and point."
Deal but with moral mathematics so—
Master one merest moment's work of mine,
Even this practising with pen and ink,—
Demonstrate why I rather plied the quill
Than left the space a blank,—you gain a fact,
And God knows what a fact 's worth! So proceed
By inference from just this moral fact
—I don't say, to that plaguy quadrature,
"What the whole man meant, whom you wish you knew,"
But, what meant certain things he did of old,
Which puzzled Europe,—why, you 'll find them plain,
This way, not otherwise: I guarantee,
Understand one, you comprehend the rest.
Rays from all round converge to any point:
Study the point then ere you track the rays!
The size o' the circle 's nothing; subdivide
Earth, and earth's smallest grain of mustard-seed,
You count as many parts, small matching large
If you can use the mind's eye: otherwise,

Material optics, being gross at best,
Prefer the large and leave our mind the small—
And pray how many folk have minds can see?
Certainly you—and somebody in Thrace
Whose name escapes me at the moment. You—
Lend me your mind then! Analyze with me
This instance of the line 'twixt blot and blot
I rather chose to draw than leave a blank,
Things else being equal. You are taught thereby
That 't is my nature, when I am at ease,
Rather than idle out my life too long,
To want to do a thing—to put a thought,
Whether a great thought or a little one,
Into an act, as nearly as may be.
Make what is absolutely new—I can't,
Mar what is made already well enough—
I won't: but turn to best account the thing
That 's half-made—that I can. Two blots, you saw
I knew how to extend into a line
Symmetric on the sheet they blurred before—
Such little act sufficed, this time, such thought.

Now, we 'll extend rays, widen out the verge,
Describe a larger circle; leave this first
Clod of an instance we began with, rise
To the complete world many clods effect.
Only continue patient while I throw,
Delver-like, spadeful after spadeful up,
Just as truths come, the subsoil of me, mould
Whence spring my moods: your object,—just to find,
Alike from handlift and from barrow-load,
What salts and silts may constitute the earth—
If it be proper stuff to blow man glass,
Or bake him pottery, bear him oaks or wheat—
What 's born of me, in brief; which found, all 's known.
If it were genius did the digging-job,
Logic would speedily sift its product smooth
And leave the crude truths bare for poetry;
But I 'm no poet, and am stiff i' the back.
What one spread fails to bring, another may.
In goes the shovel and out comes scoop—as here!

I live to please myself. I recognize
Power passing mine, immeasurable, God—
Above me, whom he made, as heaven beyond
Earth—to use figures which assist our sense.
I know that he is there as I am here,
By the same proof, which seems no proof at all,

It so exceeds familiar forms of proof.
Why "there," not "here"? Because, when I say "there"
I treat the feeling with distincter shape
That space exists between us: I,—not he,—
Live, think, do human work here—no machine,
His will moves, but a being by myself,
His, and not he who made me for a work,
Watches my working, judges its effect,
But does not interpose. He did so once,
And probably will again some time—not now,
Life being the minute of mankind, not God's,
In a certain sense, like time before and time
After man's earthly life, so far as man
Needs apprehend the matter. Am I clear?
Suppose I bid a courier take to-night—
(... Once for all, let me talk as if I smoked
Yet in the Residenz, a personage:
I must still represent the thing I was,
Galvanically make dead muscle play,
Or how shall I illustrate muscle's use?)
I could then, last July, bid courier take
Message for me, post-haste, a thousand miles.
I bid him, since I have the right to bid,
And, my part done so far, his part begins;
He starts with due equipment, will and power,
Means he may use, misuse, not use at all,
At his discretion, at his peril too.
I leave him to himself: but, journey done,
I count the minutes, call for the result
In quickness and the courier quality,
Weigh its worth, and then punish or reward
According to proved service; not before.
Meantime, he sleeps through noontide, rides till dawn,
Sticks to the straight road, tries the crooked path,
Measures and manages resource, trusts, doubts
Advisers by the wayside, does his best
At his discretion, lags or launches forth,
(He knows and I know) at his peril too.
You see? Exactly thus men stand to God:
I with my courier, God with me. Just so
I have his bidding to perform; but mind
And body, all of me, though made and meant
For that sole service, must consult, concert
With my own self and nobody beside,
How to effect the same: God helps not else.
'T is I who, with my stock of craft and strength,
Choose the directer cut across the hedge,
Or keep the foot-track that respects a crop.

Lie down and rest, rise up and ran,—live spare,
Feed free,—all that 's my business: but, arrive,
Deliver message, bring the answer back,
And make my bow, I must: then God will speak,
Praise me or haply blame as service proves.
To other men, to each and every one,
Another law! what likelier? God, perchance,
Grants each new man, by some as new a mode,
Intercommunication with himself,
Wreaking on finiteness infinitude;
By such a series of effects, gives each
Last his own imprint: old yet ever new
The process: 't is the way of Deity.
How it succeeds, he knows: I only know
That varied modes of creatureship abound,
Implying just as varied intercourse
For each with the creator of them all.
Each has his own mind and no other's mode.
What mode may yours be? I shall sympathize!
No doubt, you, good young lady that you are,
Despite a natural naughtiness or two,
Turn eyes up like a Pradier Magdalen
And see an outspread providential hand
Above the owl's-wing aigrette—guard and guide—
Visibly o'er your path, about your bed,
Through all your practisings with London-town.
It points, you go; it stays fixed, and you stop;
You quicken its procedure by a word
Spoken, a thought in silence, prayer and praise.
Well, I believe that such a hand may stoop,
And such appeals to it may stave off harm,
Pacify the grim guardian of this Square,
And stand you in good stead on quarter-day:
Quite possible in your case; not in mine.
"Ah, but I choose to make the difference,
Find the emancipation?" No, I hope!
If I deceive myself, take noon for night,
Please to become determinedly blind
To the true ordinance of human life,
Through mere presumption—that is my affair,
And truly a grave one; but as grave I think
Your affair, yours, the specially observed,—
Each favored person that perceives his path
Pointed him, inch by inch, and looks above
For guidance, through the mazes of this world,
In what we call its meanest life-career
—Not how to manage Europe properly,
But how keep open shop, and yet pay rent,

Rear household, and make both ends meet, the same.
I say, such man is no less tasked than I
To duly take the path appointed him
By whatsoever sign he recognize.
Our insincerity on both our heads!
No matter what the object of a life,
Small work or large,—the making thrive a shop,
Or seeing that an empire take no harm,—
There are known fruits to judge obedience by.
You 've read a ton's weight, now, of newspaper—
Lives of me, gabble about the kind of prince—
You know my work i' the rough; I ask you, then,
Do I appear subordinated less
To hand-impulsion, one prime push for all,
Than little lives of men, the multitude
That cried out, every quarter of an hour,
For fresh instructions, did or did not work,
And praised in the odd minutes?

Eh, my dear?
Such is the reason why I acquiesced
In doing what seemed best for me to do,
So as to please myself on the great scale,
Having regard to immortality
No less than life—did that which head and heart
Prescribed my hand, in measure with its means
Of doing—used my special stock of power—
Not from the aforesaid head and heart alone,
But every sort of helpful circumstance,
Some problematic and some nondescript:
All regulated by the single care
I' the last resort—that I made thoroughly serve
The when and how, toiled where was need, reposed
As resolutely at the proper point,
Braved sorrow, courted joy, to just one end:
Namely, that just the creature I was bound
To be, I should become, nor thwart at all
God's purpose in creation. I conceive
No other duty possible to man,—
Highest mind, lowest mind,—no other law
By which to judge life failure or success:
What folk call being saved or cast away.

Such was my rule of life; I worked my best,
Subject to ultimate judgment, God's not man's.
Well then, this settled,—take your tea, I beg,
And meditate the fact, 'twixt sip and sip,—
This settled—why I pleased myself, you saw,

By turning blot and blot into a line,
O' the little scale,—we 'll try now (as your tongue
Tries the concluding sugar-drop) what 's meant
To please me most o' the great scale. Why, just now,
With nothing else to do within my reach,
Did I prefer making two blots one line
To making yet another separate
Third blot, and leaving those I found unlinked?
It meant, I like to use the thing I find,
Rather than strive at unfound novelty:
I make the best of the old, nor try for new.
Such will to act, such choice of action's way,
Constitute—when at work on the great scale,
Driven to their farthest natural consequence
By all the help from all the means—my own
Particular faculty of serving God,
Instinct for putting power to exercise
Upon some wish and want o' the time, I prove
Possible to mankind as best I may.
This constitutes my mission,—grant the phrase,—
Namely, to rule men—men within my reach,
To order, influence and dispose them so
As render solid and stabilify
Mankind in particles, the light and loose,
For their good and my pleasure in the act.
Such good accomplished proves twice good to me—
Good for its own sake, as the just and right,
And, in the effecting also, good again
To me its agent, tasked as suits my taste.

Is this much easy to be understood
At first glance? Now begin the steady gaze!

My rank—(if I must tell you simple truth—
Telling were else not worth the whiff o' the weed
I lose for the tale's sake)—dear, my rank i' the world
Is hard to know and name precisely: err
I may, but scarcely overestimate
My style and title. Do I class with men
Most useful to their fellows? Possibly,—
Therefore, in some sort, best; but, greatest mind
And rarest nature? Evidently no.
A conservator, call me, if you please,
Not a creator nor destroyer: one
Who keeps the world safe. I profess to trace
The broken circle of society,
Dim actual order, I can redescribe
Not only where some segment silver-true

Stays clear, but where the breaks of black commence
Baffling you all who want the eye to probe—
As I make out yon problematic thin
White paring of your thumb-nail outside there,
Above the plaster-monarch on his steed—
See an inch, name an ell, and prophesy
O' the rest that ought to follow, the round moon
Now hiding in the night of things: that round,
I labor to demonstrate moon enough
For the month's purpose,—that society,
Render efficient for the age's need:
Preserving you in either case the old,
Nor aiming at a new and greater thing,
A sun for moon, a future to be made
By first abolishing the present law:
No such proud task for me by any means!
History shows you men whose master-touch
Not so much modifies as makes anew:
Minds that transmute nor need restore at all.
A breath of God made manifest in flesh
Subjects the world to change, from time to time,
Alters the whole conditions of our race
Abruptly, not by unperceived degrees
Nor play of elements already there,
But quite new leaven, leavening the lump,
And liker, so, the natural process. See!
Where winter reigned for ages—by a turn
I' the time, some star-change, (ask geologists,)
The ice-tracts split, clash, splinter and disperse,
And there 's an end of immobility,
Silence, and all that tinted pageant, base
To pinnacle, one flush from fairy-land
Dead-asleep and deserted somewhere,—see!—
As a fresh sun, wave, spring and joy outburst.
Or else the earth it is, time starts from trance,
Her mountains tremble into fire, her plains
Heave blinded by confusion: what result?
New teeming growth, surprises of strange life
Impossible before, a world, broke up
And re-made, order gained by law destroyed.
Not otherwise, in our society
Follow like portents, all as absolute
Regenerations: they have birth at rare
Uncertain unexpected intervals
O' the world, by ministry impossible
Before and after fulness of the days:
Some dervish desert-spectre, swordsman, saint,
Lawgiver, lyrist,—oh, we know the names!

Quite other these than I. Our time requires
No such strange potentate,—who else would dawn,—
No fresh force till the old have spent itself.
Such seems the natural economy.
To shoot a beam into the dark, assists:
To make that beam do fuller service, spread
And utilize such bounty to the height,
That assists also,—and that work is mine.
I recognize, contemplate, and approve
The general compact of society,
Not simply as I see effected good,
But good i' the germ, each chance that 's possible
I' the plan traced so far: all results, in short,
For better or worse of the operation due
To those exceptional natures, unlike mine,
Who, helping, thwarting, conscious, unaware,
Did somehow manage to so far describe
This diagram left ready to my hand,
Waiting my turn of trial. I see success,
See failure, see what makes or mars throughout.
How shall I else but help complete this plan
Of which I know the purpose and approve,
By letting stay therein what seems to stand,
And adding good thereto of easier reach
To-day than yesterday?

So much, no more!
Whereon, "No more than that?"—inquire aggrieved
Half of my critics: "nothing new at all?
The old plan saved, instead of a sponged slate
And fresh-drawn figure?"—while, "So much as that?"
Object their fellows of the other faith:
"Leave uneffaced the crazy labyrinth
Of alteration and amendment, lines
Which every dabster felt in duty bound
To signalize his power of pen and ink
By adding to a plan once plain enough?
Why keep each fool's bequeathment, scratch and blur
Which overscrawl and underscore the piece—
Nay, strengthen them by touches of your own?"

Well, that 's my mission, so I serve the world,
Figure as man o' the moment,—in default
Of somebody inspired to strike such change
Into society—from round to square,
The ellipsis to the rhomboid, how you please,
As suits the size and shape o' the world he finds.
But this I can,—and nobody my peer,—

Do the best with the least change possible:
Carry the incompleteness on, a stage,
Make what was crooked straight, and roughness smooth,
And weakness strong: wherein if I succeed,
It will not prove the worst achievement, sure,
In the eyes at least of one man, one I look
Nowise to catch in critic company:
To wit, the man inspired, the genius' self
Destined to come and change things thoroughly.
He, at least, finds his business simplified,
Distinguishes the done from undone, reads
Plainly what meant and did not mean this time
We live in, and I work on, and transmit
To such successor: he will operate
On good hard substance, not mere shade and shine.
Let all my critics, born to idleness
And impotency, get their good, and have
Their hooting at the giver: I am deaf—
Who find great good in this society,
Great gain, the purchase of great labor. Touch
The work I may and must, but—reverent
In every fall o' the finger-tip, no doubt.
Perhaps I find all good there 's warrant for
I' the world as yet: nay, to the end of time,—
Since evil never means part company
With mankind, only shift side and change shape.
I find advance i' the main, and notably
The Present an improvement on the Past,
And promise for the Future—which shall prove
Only the Present with its rough made smooth,
Its indistinctness emphasized; I hope
No better, nothing newer for mankind,
But something equably smoothed everywhere,
Good, reconciled with hardly-quite-as-good,
Instead of good and bad each jostling each.
"And that 's all?" Ay, and quite enough for me!
We have toiled so long to gain what gain I find
I' the Present,—let us keep it! We shall toil
So long before we gain—if gain God grant—
A Future with one touch of difference
I' the heart of things, and not their outside face,—
Let us not risk the whiff of my cigar
For Fourier, Comte, and all that ends in smoke!

This I see clearest probably of men
With power to act and influence, now alive:
Juster than they to the true state of things;
In consequence, more tolerant that, side

By side, shall co-exist and thrive alike
In the age, the various sorts of happiness
Moral, mark!—not material—moods o' the mind
Suited to man and man his opposite:
Say, minor modes of movement—hence to there,
Or thence to here, or simply round about—
So long as each toe spares its neighbor's kibe,
Nor spoils the major march and main advance.
The love of peace, care for the family,
Contentment with what 's bad but might be worse—
Good movements these! and good, too, discontent,
So long as that spurs good, which might be best,
Into becoming better, anyhow:
Good—pride of country, putting hearth and home
I' the background, out of undue prominence:
Good—yearning after change, strife, victory,
And triumph. Each shall have its orbit marked,
But no more,—none impede the other's path
In this wide world,—though each and all alike,
Save for me, fain would spread itself through space
And leave its fellow not an inch of way.
I rule and regulate the course, excite,
Restrain: because the whole machine should march
Impelled by those diversely-moving parts,
Each blind to aught beside its little bent.
Out of the turnings round and round inside,
Comes that straightforward world-advance, I want,
And none of them supposes God wants too
And gets through just their hindrance and my help.
I think that to have held the balance straight
For twenty years, say, weighing claim and claim
And giving each its due, no less no more,
This was good service to humanity,
Right usage of my power in head and heart,
And reasonable piety beside.
Keep those three points in mind while judging me!
You stand, perhaps, for some one man, not men,—
Represent this or the other interest,
Nor mind the general welfare,—so, impugn
My practice and dispute my value: why?
You man of faith, I did not tread the world
Into a paste, and thereof make a smooth
Uniform mound whereon to plant your flag,
The lily-white, above the blood and brains!
Nor yet did I, you man of faithlessness,
So roll things to the level which you love,
That you could stand at ease there and survey
The universal Nothing undisgraced

By pert obtrusion of some old church-spire
I' the distance! Neither friend would I content,
Nor, as the world were simply meant for him,
Thrust out his fellow and mend God's mistake.
Why, you two fools,—my dear friends all the same,—
Is it some change o' the world and nothing else
Contents you? Should whatever was, not be?
How thanklessly you view things! There 's the root
Of the evil, source of the entire mistake:
You see no worth i' the world, nature and life,
Unless we change what is to what may be,
Which means,—may be, i' the brain of one of you!
"Reject what is?"—all capabilities—
Nay, you may style them chances if you choose—
All chances, then, of happiness that lie
Open to anybody that is born,
Tumbles into this life and out again,—
All that may happen, good and evil too,
I' the space between, to each adventurer
Upon this 'sixty, Anno Domini:
A life to live—and such a life! a world
To learn, one's lifetime in,—and such a world!
How did the foolish ever pass for wise
By calling life a burden, man a fly
Or worm or what 's most insignificant?
"O littleness of man!" deplores the bard;
And then, for fear the Powers should punish him,
"O grandeur of the visible universe
Our human littleness contrasts withal!
O sun, O moon, ye mountains and thou sea,
Thou emblem of immensity, thou this,
That and the other,—what impertinence
In man to eat and drink and walk about
And have his little notions of his own,
The while some wave sheds foam upon the shore!"
First of all, 't is a lie some three-times thick:
The bard,—this sort of speech being poetry,—
The bard puts mankind well outside himself
And then begins instructing them: "This way
I and my friend the sea conceive of you!
What would you give to think such thoughts as ours
Of you and the sea together?" Down they go
On the humbled knees of them: at once they draw
Distinction, recognize no mate of theirs
In one, despite his mock humility,
So plain a match for what he plays with. Next,
The turn of the great ocean-playfellow,
When the bard, leaving Bond Street very far

From ear-shot, cares not to ventriloquize,
But tells the sea its home-truths: "You, my match?
You, all this terror and immensity
And what not? Shall I tell you what you are?
Just fit to hitch into a stanza, so
Wake up and set in motion who 's asleep
O' the other side of you in England, else
Unaware, as folk pace their Bond Street now,
Somebody here despises them so much!
Between us,—they are the ultimate! to them
And their perception go these lordly thoughts:
Since what were ocean—mane and tail, to boot—
Mused I not here, how make thoughts thinkable?
Start forth my stanza and astound the world!
Back, billows, to your insignificance!
Deep, you are done with!"

Learn, my gifted friend,
There are two things i' the world, still wiser folk
Accept—intelligence and sympathy.
You pant about unutterable power
I' the ocean, all you feel but cannot speak?
Why, that 's the plainest speech about it all.
You did not feel what was not to be felt.
Well, then, all else but what man feels is naught—
The wash o' the liquor that o'erbrims the cup
Called man, and runs to waste adown his side,
Perhaps to feed a cataract,—who cares?
I 'll tell you: all the more I know mankind,
The more I thank God, like my grandmother,
For making me a little lower than
The angels, honor-clothed and glory-crowned:
This is the honor,—that no thing I know,
Feel or conceive, but I can make my own
Somehow, by use of hand or head or heart:
This is the glory,—that in all conceived,
Or felt or known, I recognize a mind
Not mine but like mine,—for the double joy,—
Making all things for me and me for Him.
There 's folly for you at this time of day!
So think it! and enjoy your ignorance
Of what—no matter for the worthy's name—
Wisdom set working in a noble heart,
When he, who was earth's best geometer
Up to that time of day, consigned his life
With its results into one matchless book,
The triumph of the human mind so far,
All in geometry man yet could do:

And then wrote on the dedication-page
In place of name the universe applauds,
"But, God, what a geometer art Thou!"
I suppose Heaven is, through Eternity,
The equalizing, ever and anon,
In momentary rapture, great with small,
Omniscience with intelligency, God
With man,—the thunder-glow from pole to pole
Abolishing, a blissful moment-space,
Great cloud alike and small cloud, in one fire—
As sure to ebb as sure again to flow
When the new receptivity deserves
The new completion. There 's the Heaven for me.
And I say, therefore, to live out one's life
I' the world here, with the chance,—whether by pain
Or pleasure be the process, long or short
The time, august or mean the circumstance
To human eye,—of learning how set foot
Decidedly on some one path to Heaven,
Touch segment in the circle whence all lines
Lead to the centre equally, red lines
Or black lines, so they but produce themselves—
This, I do say,—and here my sermon ends,—
This makes it worth our while to tenderly
Handle a state of things which mend we might,
Mar we may, but which meanwhile helps so far.
Therefore my end is—save society!

"And that 's all?" twangs the never-failing taunt
O' the foe—"No novelty, creativeness,
Mark of the master that renews the age?"
"Nay, all that?" rather will demur my judge
I look to hear some day, nor friend nor foe—
"Did you attain, then, to perceive that God
Knew what he undertook when he made things?"
Ay: that my task was to co-operate
Rather than play the rival, chop and change
The order whence comes all the good we know,
With this,—good's last expression to our sense,—
That there 's a further good conceivable
Beyond the utmost earth can realize:
And, therefore, that to change the agency,
The evil whereby good is brought about—
Try to make good do good as evil does—
Were just as if a chemist, wanting white,
And knowing black ingredients bred the dye,
Insisted these too should be white forsooth!
Correct the evil, mitigate your best,

Blend mild with harsh, and soften black to gray
If gray may follow with no detriment
To the eventual perfect purity!
But as for hazarding the main result
By hoping to anticipate one half
In the intermediate process,—no, my friends!
This bad world, I experience and approve;
Your good world,—with no pity, courage, hope,
Fear, sorrow, joy,—devotedness, in short,
Which I account the ultimate of man,
Of which there 's not one day nor hour but brings,
In flower or fruit, some sample of success,
Out of this same society I save—
None of it for me! That I might have none,
I rapped your tampering knuckles twenty years,
Such was the task imposed me, such my end.

Now for the means thereto. Ah, confidence—
Keep we together or part company?
This is the critical minute! "Such my end?"
Certainly; how could it be otherwise?
Can there be question which was the right task—
To save or to destroy society?
Why, even prove that, by some miracle,
Destruction were the proper work to choose,
And that a torch best remedies what 's wrong
I' the temple, whence the long procession wound
Of powers and beauties, earth's achievements all,
The human strength that strove and overthrew,—
The human love that, weak itself, crowned strength,—
The instinct crying, "God is whence I came!"—
The reason laying down the law, "And such
His will i' the world must be!"—the leap and shout
Of genius, "For I hold his very thoughts,
The meaning of the mind of him!"—nay, more
The ingenuities, each active force
That turning in a circle on itself
Looks neither up nor down but keeps the spot,
Mere creature-like and, for religion, works,
Works only and works ever, makes and shapes
And changes, still wrings more of good from less,
Still stamps some bad out, where was worst before,
So leaves the handiwork, the act and deed,
Were it but house and land and wealth, to show
Here was a creature perfect in the kind—
Whether as bee, beaver, or behemoth,
What 's the importance? he has done his work
For work's sake, worked well, earned a creature's praise;—

I say, concede that same fane, whence deploys
Age after age, all this humanity,
Diverse but ever dear, out of the dark
Behind the altar into the broad day
By the portal—enter, and, concede there mocks
Each lover of free motion and much space
A perplexed length of apse and aisle and nave,—
Pillared roof and carved screen, and what care I?—
Which irk the movement and impede the march,—
Nay, possibly, bring flat upon his nose
At some odd breakneck angle, by some freak
Of old-world artistry, that personage
Who, could he but have kept his skirts from grief
And catching at the hooks and crooks about,
Had stepped out on the daylight of our time
Plainly the man of the age,—still, still, I bar
Excessive conflagration in the case.
"Shake the flame freely!" shout the multitude:
The architect approves I stuck my torch
Inside a good stout lantern, hung its light
Above the hooks and crooks, and ended so.
To save society was well: the means
Whereby to save it,—there begins the doubt
Permitted you, imperative on me;
Were mine the best means? Did I work aright
With powers appointed me?—since powers denied
Concern me nothing.

Well, my work reviewed
Fairly, leaves more hope than discouragement.
First, there 's the deed done: what I found, I leave,—
What tottered, I kept stable: if it stand
One month, without sustainment, still thank me
The twenty years' sustainer! Now, observe,
Sustaining is no brilliant self-display
Like knocking down or even setting up:
Much bustle these necessitate; and still
To vulgar eye, the mightier of the myth
Is Hercules, who substitutes his own
For Atlas' shoulder and supports the globe
A whole day,—not the passive and obscure
Atlas who bore, ere Hercules was born,
And is to go on bearing that same load
When Hercules turns ash on Œta's top.
'T is the transition-stage, the tug and strain.
That strike men: standing still is stupid-like,
My pressure was too constant on the whole
For any part's eruption into space

'Mid sparkles, crackling, and much praise of me.
I saw that, in the ordinary life,
Many of the little make a mass of men
Important beyond greatness here and there;
As certainly as, in life exceptional,
When old things terminate and new commence,
A solitary great man 's worth the world.
God takes the business into his own hands
At such time: who creates the novel flower
Contrives to guard and give it breathing-room:
I merely tend the cornfield, care for crop,
And weed no acre thin to let emerge
What prodigy may stifle there perchance,
—No, though my eye have noted where he lurks.
Oh those mute myriads that spoke loud to me—
The eyes that craved to see the light, the mouths
That sought the daily bread and nothing more,
The hands that supplicated exercise,
Men that had wives, and women that had babes,
And all these making suit to only live!
Was I to turn aside from husbandry,
Leave hope of harvest for the corn, my care,
To play at horticulture, rear some rose
Or poppy into perfect leaf and bloom
When, 'mid the furrows, up was pleased to sprout
Some man, cause, system, special interest
I ought to study, stop the world meanwhile?
"But I am Liberty, Philanthropy,
Enlightenment, or Patriotism, the power
Whereby you are to stand or fall!" cries each:
"Mine and mine only be the flag you flaunt!"
And, when I venture to object, "Meantime,
What of yon myriads with no flag at all—
My crop which, who flaunts flag must tread across?"
"Now, this it is to have a puny mind!"
Admire my mental prodigies: "down—down—
Ever at home o' the level and the low,
There hides he brooding! Could he look above,
With less of the owl and more of the eagle eye,
He 'd see there 's no way helps the little cause
Like the attainment of the great. Dare first
The chief emprise; dispel yon cloud between
The sun and us; nor fear that, though our heads
Find earlier warmth and comfort from his ray,
What lies about our feet, the multitude,
Will fail of benefaction presently.
Come now, let each of us awhile cry truce
To special interests, make common cause

Against the adversary—or perchance
Mere dullard to his own plain interest!
Which of us will you choose?—since needs must be
Some one o' the warring causes you incline
To hold, i' the main, has right and should prevail:
Why not adopt and give it prevalence?
Choose strict Faith or lax Incredulity,—
King, Caste, and Cultus—or the Rights of Man,
Sovereignty of each Proudhon o'er himself,
And all that follows in just consequence!
Go free the stranger from a foreign yoke;
Or stay, concentrate energy at home;
Succeed!—when he deserves, the stranger will.
Comply with the Great Nation's impulse, print
By force of arms,—since reason pleads in vain,
And, 'mid the sweet compulsion, pity weeps,—
Hohenstiel-Schwangau on the universe!
Snub the Great Nation, cure the impulsive itch
With smartest fillip on a restless nose
Was ever launched by thumb and finger! Bid
Hohenstiel-Schwangau first repeal the tax
On pig-tails and pomatum, and then mind
Abstruser matters for next century!
Is your choice made? Why then, act up to choice!
Leave the illogical touch now here now there
I' the way of work, the tantalizing help
First to this, then the other opposite:
The blowing hot and cold, sham policy,
Sure ague of the mind and nothing more,
Disease of the perception or the will,
That fain would hide in a fine name! Your choice,
Speak it out and condemn yourself thereby!"

Well, Leicester Square is not the Residenz:
Instead of shrugging shoulder, turning friend
The deaf ear, with a wink to the police—
I 'll answer—by a question, wisdom's mode.
How many years, o' the average, do men
Live in this world? Some score, say computists.
Quintuple me that term and give mankind
The likely hundred, and with all my heart
I 'll take your task upon me, work your way,
Concentrate energy on some one cause:
Since, counseller, I also have my cause,
My flag, my faith in its effect, my hope
In its eventual triumph for the good
O' the world. And once upon a time, when I
Was like all you, mere voice and nothing more,

Myself took wings, soared sunward, and thence sang,
"Look where I live i' the loft, come up to me,
Groundlings, nor grovel longer! gain this height,
And prove you breathe here better than below!
Why, what emancipation far and wide
Will follow in a trice! They too can soar,
Each tenant of the earth's circumference
Claiming to elevate humanity,
They also must attain such altitude,
Live in the luminous circle that surrounds
The planet, not the leaden orb itself.
Press out, each point, from surface to yon verge
Which one has gained and guaranteed your realm!"
Ay, still my fragments wander, music-fraught,
Sighs of the soul, mine once, mine now, and mine
Forever! Crumbled arch, crushed aqueduct.
Alive with tremors in the shaggy growth
Of wild-wood, crevice-sown, that triumphs there
Imparting exultation to the hills!
Sweep of the swathe when only the winds walk
And waft my words above the grassy sea
Under the blinding blue that basks o'er Rome,—
Hear ye not still—"Be Italy again"?
And ye, what strikes the panic to your heart?
Decrepit council-chambers,—where some lamp
Drives the unbroken black three paces off
From where the graybeards huddle in debate,
Dim cowls and capes, and midmost glimmers one
Like tarnished gold, and what they say is doubt,
And what they think is fear, and what suspends
The breath in them is not the plaster-patch
Time disengages from the painted wall
Where Rafael moulderingly bids adieu,
Nor tick of the insect turning tapestry
Which a queen's finger traced of old, to dust;
But some word, resonant, redoubtable,
Of who once felt upon his head a hand
Whereof the head now apprehends his foot.
"Light in Rome, Law in Rome, and Liberty
O' the soul in Rome—the free Church, the free State!
Stamp out the nature that's best typified
By its embodiment in Peter's Dome,
The scorpion-body with the greedy pair
Of outstretched nippers, either colonnade
Agape for the advance of heads and hearts!"
There 's one cause for you! one and only one,
For I am vocal through the universe,
I' the workshop, manufactory, exchange

And market-place, seaport and custom-house
O' the frontier: listen if the echoes die—
"Unfettered commerce! Power to speak and hear,
And print and read! The universal vote!
Its rights for labor!" This, with much beside,
I spoke when I was voice and nothing more,
But altogether such an one as you
My censors. "Voice, and nothing more, indeed!"
Re-echoes round me: "that 's the censure, there 's
Involved the ruin of you soon or late!
Voice,—when its promise beat the empty air:
And nothing more,—when solid earth's your stage,
And we desiderate performance, deed
For word, the realizing all you dreamed
In the old days: now, for deed, we find at door
O' the council-chamber posted, mute as mouse,
Hohenstiel-Schwangau, sentry and safeguard
O' the graybeards all a-chuckle, cowl to cape,
Who challenge Judas,—that 's endearment's style,—
To stop their mouths or let escape grimace,
While they keep cursing Italy and him.
The power to speak, hear, print and read is ours?
Ay, we learn where and how, when clapped inside
A convict-transport bound for cool Cayenne!
The universal vote we have: its urn,
We also have where votes drop, fingered-o'er
By the universal Prefect. Say, Trade 's free
And Toil turned master out o' the slave it was:
What then? These feed man's stomach, but his soul
Craves finer fare, nor lives by bread alone,
As somebody says somewhere. Hence you stand
Proved and recorded either false or weak,
Faulty in promise or performance: which?"
Neither, I hope. Once pedestalled on earth,
To act not speak, I found earth was not air.
I saw that multitude of mine, and not
The nakedness and nullity of air
Fit only for a voice to float in free.
Such eyes I saw that craved the light alone,
Such mouths that wanted bread and nothing else,
Such hands that supplicated handiwork,
Men with the wives, and women with the babes,
Yet all these pleading just to live, not die!
Did I believe one whit less in belief,
Take truth for falsehood, wish the voice revoked
That told the truth to heaven for earth to hear?
No, this should be, and shall; but when and how?
At what expense to these who average

Your twenty years of life, my computists?
"Not bread alone," but bread before all else
For these: the bodily want serve first, said I;
If earth-space and the lifetime help not here,
Where is the good of body having been?
But, helping body, if we somewhat balk
The soul of finer fare, such food 's to find
Elsewhere and afterward—all indicates,
Even this selfsame fact that soul can starve
Yet body still exist its twenty years:
While, stint the body, there 's an end at once
O' the revel in the fancy that Rome 's free,
And superstition's fettered, and one prints
Whate'er one pleases, and who pleases reads
The same, and speaks out and is spoken to,
And divers hundred thousand fools may vote
A vote untampered with by one wise man,
And so elect Barabbas deputy
In lieu of his concurrent. I who trace
The purpose written on the face of things,
For my behoof and guidance—(whoso needs
No such sustainment, sees beneath my signs,
Proves, what I take for writing, penmanship,
Scribble and flourish with no sense for me
O' the sort I solemnly go spelling out,—
Let him! there 's certain work of mine to show
Alongside his work: which gives warranty
Of shrewder vision in the workman—judge!)
I who trace Providence without a break
I' the plan of things, drop plumb on this plain print
Of an intention with a view to good,
That man is made in sympathy with man
At outset of existence, so to speak;
But in dissociation, more and more,
Man from his fellow, as their lives advance
In culture; still humanity, that 's born
A mass, keeps flying off, fining away
Ever into a multitude of points,
And ends in isolation, each from each:
Peerless above i' the sky, the pinnacle,—
Absolute contact, fusion, all below
At the base of being. How comes this about?
This stamp of God characterizing man
And nothing else but man in the universe—
That, while he feels with man (to use man's speech)
I' the little things of life, its fleshly wants
Of food and rest and health and happiness,
Its simplest spirit-motions, loves and hates,

Hopes, fears, soul-cravings on the ignoblest scale,
O' the fellow-creature,—owns the bond at base,—
He tends to freedom and divergency
In the upward progress, plays the pinnacle
When life 's at greatest (grant again the phrase!
Because there 's neither great nor small in life).
"Consult thou for thy kind that have the eyes
To see, the mouths to eat, the hands to work,
Men with the wives, and women with the babes!"
Prompts Nature. "Care thou for thyself alone
I' the conduct of the mind God made thee with!
Think, as if man had never thought before!
Act, as if all creation hung attent
On the acting of such faculty as thine,
To take prime pattern from thy masterpiece!"
Nature prompts also: neither law obeyed
To the uttermost by any heart and soul
We know or have in record: both of them
Acknowledged blindly by whatever man
We ever knew or heard of in this world.
"Will you have why and wherefore, and the fact
Made plain as pikestaff?" modern Science asks.
"That mass man sprung from was a jelly-lump
Once on a time; he kept an after-course
Through fish and insect, reptile, bird and beast,
Till he attained to be an ape at last
Or last but one. And if this doctrine shock
In aught the natural pride" ... Friend, banish fear,
The natural humility replies.
Do you suppose, even I, poor potentate,
Hohenstiel-Schwangau, who once ruled the roast,—
I was born able at all points to ply
My tools? or did I have to learn my trade,
Practise as exile ere perform as prince?
The world knows something of my ups and downs:
But grant me time, give me the management
And manufacture of a model me,
Me fifty-fold, a prince without a flaw,—
Why, there 's no social grade, the sordidest,
My embryo potentate should blink and 'scape.
King, all the better he was cobbler once,
He should know, sitting on the throne, how tastes
Life to who sweeps the doorway. But life 's hard,
Occasion rare; you cut probation short,
And, being half-instructed, on the stage
You shuffle through your part as best you can,
And bless your stars, as I do. God takes time.
I like the thought he should have lodged me once

I' the hole, the cave, the hut, the tenement,
The mansion and the palace; made me learn
The feel o' the first, before I found myself
Loftier i' the last, not more emancipate;
From first to last of lodging, I was I,
And not at all the place that harbored me.
Do I refuse to follow farther yet
I' the backwardness, repine if tree and flower,
Mountain or streamlet were my dwelling-place
Before I gained enlargement, grew mollusc?
As well account that way for many a thrill
Of kinship, I confess to, with the powers
Called Nature: animate, inanimate,
In parts or in the whole, there 's something there
Man-like that somehow meets the man in me.
My pulse goes altogether with the heart
O' the Persian, that old Xerxes, when he stayed
His march to conquest of the world, a day
I' the desert, for the sake of one superb
Plane-tree which queened it there in solitude:
Giving her neck its necklace, and each arm
Its armlet, suiting soft waist, snowy side,
With cincture and apparel. Yes, I lodged
In those successive tenements; perchance
Taste yet the straitness of them while I stretch
Limb and enjoy new liberty the more.
And some abodes are lost or ruinous;
Some, patched-up and pieced-out, and so transformed
They still accommodate the traveller
His day of lifetime. Oh, you count the links,
Descry no bar of the unbroken man?
Yes,—and who welds a lump of ore, suppose
He likes to make a chain and not a bar,
And reach by link on link, link small, link large,
Out to the due length—why, there 's forethought still
Outside o' the series, forging at one end,
While at the other there 's—no matter what
The kind of critical intelligence
Believing that last link had last but one
For parent, and no link was, first of all,
Fitted to anvil, hammered into shape.
Else, I accept the doctrine, and deduce
This duty, that I recognize mankind,
In all its height and depth and length and breadth.
Mankind i' the main have little wants, not large:
I, being of will and power to help, i' the main,
Mankind, must help the least wants first. My friend,
That is, my foe, without such power and will,

May plausibly concentrate all he wields,
And do his best at helping some large want,
Exceptionally noble cause, that's seen
Subordinate enough from where I stand.
As he helps, I helped once, when like himself,
Unable to help better, work more wide;
And so would work with heart and hand to-day;
Did only computists confess a fault,
And multiply the single score by five,
Five only, give man's life its hundred years.
Change life, in me shall follow change to match!
Time were then, to work here, there, everywhere,
By turns and try experiment at ease!
Full time to mend as well as mar: why wait
The slow and sober uprise all around
O' the building? Let us run up, right to roof,
Some sudden marvel, piece of perfectness,
And testify what we intend the whole!
Is the world losing patience? "Wait!" say we:
"There 's time: no generation needs to die
Unsolaced; you 've a century in store!"
But, no: I sadly let the voices wing
Their way i' the upper vacancy, nor test
Truth on this solid as I promised once.
Well, and what is there to be sad about?
The world 's the world, life 's life, and nothing else.
'T is part of life, a property to prize,
That those o' the higher sort engaged i' the world,
Should fancy they can change its ill to good,
Wrong to right, ugliness to beauty: find
Enough success in fancy turning fact,
To keep the sanguine kind in countenance
And justify the hope that busies them:
Failure enough,—to who can follow change
Beyond their vision, see new good prove ill
I' the consequence, see blacks and whites of life
Shift square indeed, but leave the checkered face
Unchanged i' the main,—failure enough for such,
To bid ambition keep the whole from change,
As their best service. I hope naught beside.
No, my brave thinkers, whom I recognize,
Gladly, myself the first, as, in a sense,
All that our world 's worth, flower and fruit of man!
Such minds myself award supremacy
Over the common insignificance,
When only Mind 's in question,—Body bows
To quite another government, you know.
Be Kant crowned king o' the castle in the air!

Hans Slouch—his own, and children's mouths to feed
I' the hovel on the ground—wants meat, nor chews
"The Critique of Pure Reason" in exchange.
But, now,—suppose I could allow your claims
And quite change life to please you,—would it please?
Would life comport with change and still be life?
Ask, now, a doctor for a remedy:
There 's his prescription. Bid him point you out
Which of the five or six ingredients saves
The sick man. "Such the efficacity?
Then why not dare and do things in one dose
Simple and pure, all virtue, no alloy
Of the idle drop and powder?" What 's his word?
The efficacity, neat, were neutralized:
It wants dispersing and retarding,—nay,
Is put upon its mettle, plays its part
Precisely through such hindrance everywhere,
Finds some mysterious give and take i' the case.
Some gain by opposition, he foregoes
Should he unfetter the medicament.
So with this thought of yours that fain would work
Free in the world: it wants just what it finds—
The ignorance, stupidity, the hate,
Envy and malice and uncharitableness
That bar your passage, break the flow of you
Down from those happy heights where many a cloud
Combined to give you birth and bid you be
The royalest of rivers: on you glide
Silverly till you reach the summit-edge,
Then over, on to all that ignorance,
Stupidity, hate, envy, bluffs and blocks,
Posted to fret you into foam and noise.
What of it? Up you mount in minute mist,
And bridge the chasm that, crushed your quietude,
A spirit-rainbow, earthborn jewelry
Outsparkling the insipid firmament
Blue above Terni and its orange-trees.
Do not mistake me! You, too, have your rights!
Hans must not burn Kant's house above his head
Because he cannot understand Kant's book:
And still less must Hans' pastor burn Kant's self
Because Kant understands some books too well.
But, justice seen to on this little point,
Answer me, is it manly, is it sage
To stop and struggle with arrangements here
It took so many lives, so much of toil,
To tinker up into efficiency?
Can't you contrive to operate at once,—

Since time is short and art is long,—to show
Your quality i' the world, whate'er you boast,
Without this fractious call on folks to crush
The world together just to set you free,
Admire the capers you will cut perchance,
Nor mind the mischief to your neighbors?

"Age!
Age and experience bring discouragement,"
You taunt me: I maintain the opposite.
Am I discouraged who—perceiving health,
Strength, beauty, as they tempt the eye of soul,
Are uncombinable with flesh and blood—
Resolve to let my body live its best,
And leave my soul what better yet may be
Or not be, in this life or afterward?
—In either fortune, wiser than who waits
Till magic art procure a miracle.
In virtue of my very confidence
Mankind ought to outgrow its babyhood;
I prescribe rocking, deprecate rough hands,
While thus the cradle holds it past mistake.
Indeed, my task 's the harder—equable
Sustainment everywhere, all strain, no push—
Whereby friends credit me with indolence,
Apathy, hesitation. "Stand stock-still
If able to move briskly? 'All a-strain'—
So must we compliment your passiveness?
Sound asleep, rather!"

Just the judgment passed
Upon a statue, luckless like myself,
I saw at Rome once! 'T was some artist's whim
To cover all the accessories close
I' the group, and leave you only Laocoön
With neither sons nor serpents to denote
The purpose of his gesture. Then a crowd
Was called to try the question, criticise
Wherefore such energy of legs and arms,
Nay, eyeballs, starting from the socket. One—
I give him leave to write my history—
Only one said, "I think the gesture strives
Against some obstacle we cannot see."
All the rest made their minds up. "'T is a yawn
Of sheer fatigue subsiding to repose:
The statue 's 'Somnolency' clear enough!"

There, my arch stranger-friend, my audience both

And arbitress, you have one half your wish,
At least: you know the thing I tried to do!
All, so far, to my praise and glory—all
Told as befits the self-apologist,—
Who ever promises a candid sweep
And clearance of those errors miscalled crimes
None knows more, none laments so much as he,
And ever rises from confession, proved
A god whose fault was—trying to be man.
Just so, fair judge,—if I read smile aright—
I condescend to figure in your eyes
As biggest heart and best of Europe's friends,
And hence my failure. God will estimate
Success one day; and, in the mean time—you!

I daresay there 's some fancy of the sort
Frolicking round this final puff I send
To die up yonder in the ceiling-rose,—
Some consolation-stakes, we losers win!
A plague of the return to "I—I—I
Did this, meant that, hoped, feared the other thing!"
Autobiography, adieu! The rest
Shall make amends, be pure blame, history
And falsehood: not the ineffective truth,
But Thiers-and-Victor-Hugo exercise.
Hear what I never was, but might have been
I' the better world where goes tobacco-smoke!
Here lie the dozen volumes of my life:
(Did I say "lie"? the pregnant word will serve.)
Cut on to the concluding chapter, though!
Because the little hours begin to strike.
Hurry Thiers-Hugo to the labor's end!

Something like this the unwritten chapter reads.

Exemplify the situation thus!
Hohenstiel-Schwangau, being, no dispute,
Absolute mistress, chose the Assembly, first,
To serve her: chose this man, its President
Afterward, to serve also,—specially
To see that folk did service one and all.
And now the proper term of years was out,
When the Head-servant must vacate his place;
And nothing lay so patent to the world
As that his fellow-servants one and all
Were—mildly to make mention—knaves or fools,
Each of them with his promise flourished full
I' the face of you by word and impudence,

Or filtered slyly out by nod and wink
And nudge upon your sympathetic rib—
That not one minute more did knave or fool
Mean to keep faith and serve as he had sworn
Hohenstiel-Schwangau, once her Head away.
Why should such swear except to get the chance,
When time should ripen and confusion bloom,
Of putting Hohenstielers-Schwangauese
To the true use of human property—
Restoring souls and bodies, this to Pope,
And that to King, that other to his planned
Perfection of a Share-and-share-alike,
That other still, to Empire absolute
In shape of the Head-servant's very self
Transformed to Master whole and sole? each scheme
Discussible, concede one circumstance—
That each scheme's parent were, beside himself,
Hohenstiel-Schwangau, not her serving-man
Sworn to do service in the way she chose
Rather than his way: way superlative,
Only,—by some infatuation,—his
And his and his and every one's but hers
Who stuck to just the Assembly and the Head.
I make no doubt the Head, too, had his dream
Of doing sudden duty swift and sure
On all that heap of untrustworthiness—
Catching each vaunter of the villany
He meant to perpetrate when time was ripe,
Once the Head-servant fairly out of doors,—
And, caging here a knave and there a fool,
Cry, "Mistress of your servants, these and me,
Hohenstiel-Schwangau! I, their trusty Head,
Pounce on a pretty scheme concocting here
That's stopped, extinguished by my vigilance.
Your property is safe again: but mark!
Safe in these hands, not yours, who lavish trust
Too lightly. Leave my hands their charge awhile!
I know your business better than yourself:
Let me alone about it! Some fine day,
Once we are rid of the embarrassment,
You shall look up and see your longings crowned!"
Such fancy might have tempted him be false,
But this man chose truth and was wiser so.
He recognized that for great minds i' the world
There is no trial like the appropriate one
Of leaving little minds their liberty
Of littleness to blunder on through life,
Now aiming at right ends by foolish means,

Now, at absurd achievement through the aid
Of good and wise endeavor—to acquiesce
In folly's life-long privilege, though with power
To do the little minds the good they need,
Despite themselves, by just abolishing
Their right to play the part and fill the place
I' the scheme of things He schemed who made alike
Great minds and little minds, saw use for each.
Could the orb sweep those puny particles
It just half-lights at distance, hardly leads
I' the leash—sweep out each speck of them from space
They anticise in with their days and nights
And whirlings round and dancings off, forsooth,
And all that fruitless individual life
One cannot lend a beam to but they spoil—
Sweep them into itself and so, one star,
Preponderate henceforth i' the heritage
Of heaven! No! in less senatorial phrase,
The man endured to help, not save outright
The multitude by substituting him
For them, his knowledge, will and way, for God's:
Nor change the world, such as it is, and was
And will be, for some other, suiting all
Except the purpose of the maker. No!
He saw that weakness, wickedness will be,
And therefore should be: that the perfect man,
As we account perfection—at most pure
O' the special gold, whate'er the form it take,
Head-work or heart-work, fined and thrice-refined
I' the crucible of life, whereto the powers
Of the refiner, one and all, are flung
To feed the flame, he saw that e'en the block,
Such perfect man holds out triumphant, breaks
Into some poisonous ore, gold's opposite,
At the very purest, so compensating
Man's Adversary—what if we believe?
For earlier stern exclusion of his stuff.
See the sage, with the hunger for the truth,
And see his system that's all true, except
The one weak place that's stanchioned by a lie!
The moralist, who walks with head erect
I' the crystal clarity of air so long,
Until a stumble, and the man's one mire!
Philanthropy undoes the social knot
With axe-edge, makes love room 'twixt head and trunk:
Religion—but, enough, the thing's too clear!
Well, if these sparks break out i' the greenest tree,
Our topmost of performance, yours and mine,

What will be done i' the dry ineptitude
Of ordinary mankind, bark and bole,
All seems ashamed of but their mother-earth?
Therefore throughout Head's term of servitude
He did the appointed service, and forebore
Extraneous action that were duty else,
Done by some other servant, idle now
Or mischievous: no matter, each his own—
Own task, and, in the end, own praise or blame!
He suffered them strut, prate, and brag their best,
Squabble at odds on every point save one,
And there shake hands,—agree to trifle time,
Obstruct advance with, each, his cricket-cry,
"Wait till the Head be off the shoulders here!
Then comes my King, my Pope, my Autocrat,
My Socialist Republic to her own—
To-wit, that property of only me,
Hohenstiel-Schwangau who conceits herself
Free, forsooth, and expects I keep her so!"
—Nay, suffered when, perceiving with dismay
Head's silence paid no tribute to their noise,
They turned on him. "Dumb menace in that mouth,
Malice in that unstridulosity!
He cannot but intend some stroke of state
Shall signalize his passage into peace
Out of the creaking,—hinder transference
O' the Hohenstielers-Schwangauese to king,
Pope, autocrat, or socialist republic! That 's
Exact the cause his lips unlocked would cry!
Therefore be stirring: brave, beard, bully him!
Dock, by the million, of its friendly joints,
The electoral body short at once! who did,
May do again, and undo us beside;
Wrest from his hands the sword for self-defence,
The right to parry any thrust in play
We peradventure please to meditate!"
And so forth; creak, creak, creak: and ne'er a line
His locked mouth oped the wider, till at last
O' the long degraded and insulting day,
Sudden the clock told it was judgment-time.
Then he addressed himself to speak indeed
To the fools, not knaves: they saw him walk straight down
Each step of the eminence, as he first engaged,
And stand at last o' the level,—all he swore.
"People, and not the people's varletry,
This is the task you set myself and these!
Thus I performed my part of it, and thus
They thwarted me throughout, here, here and here:

Study each instance! yours the loss, not mine.
What they intend now is demonstrable
As plainly: here's such man, and here's such mode
Of making you some other than the thing
You, wisely or unwisely, choose to be,
And only set him up to keep you so.
Do you approve this? Yours the loss, not mine.
Do you condemn it? There 's a remedy.
Take me—who know your mind, and mean your good.
With clearer brain and stouter arm than they,
Or you, or haply anybody else—
And make me master for the moment! Choose
What time, what power you trust me with: I too
Will choose as frankly ere I trust myself
With time and power: they must be adequate
To the end and aim, since mine the loss, with yours,
If means be wanting; once their worth approved,
Grant them, and I shall forthwith operate—
Ponder it well!—to the extremist stretch
O' the power you trust me: if with unsuccess,
God wills it, and there 's nobody to blame."

Whereon the people answered with a shout,
"The trusty one! no tricksters any more!"
How could they other? He was in his place.

What followed? Just what he foresaw, what proved
The soundness of both judgments,—his, o' the knaves
And fools, each trickster with his dupe,—and theirs,
The people's, in what head and arm could help.
There was uprising, masks dropped, flags unfurled,
Weapons outflourished in the wind, my faith!
Heavily did he let his fist fall plumb
On each perturber of the public peace,
No matter whose the wagging head it broke—
From bald-pate craft and greed and impudence
Of night-hawk at first chance to prowl and prey
For glory and a little gain beside,
Passing for eagle in the dusk of the age,—
To florid head-top, foamy patriotism
And tribunitial daring, breast laid bare
Through confidence in rectitude, with hand
On private pistol in the pocket: these
And all the dupes of these, who lent themselves
As dust and feather do, to help offence
O' the wind that whirls them at you, then subsides
In safety somewhere, leaving filth afloat,
Annoyance you may brush from eyes and beard,—

These he stopped: bade the wind's spite howl or whine
Its worst outside the building, wind conceives
Meant to be pulled together and become
Its natural playground so. What foolishness
Of dust or feather proved importunate
And fell 'twixt thumb and finger, found them gripe
To detriment of bulk and buoyancy.
Then followed silence and submission. Next,
The inevitable comment came on work
And work's cost: he was censured as profuse
Of human life and liberty: too swift
And thorough his procedure, who had lagged
At the outset, lost the opportunity
Through timid scruples as to right and wrong.
"There 's no such certain mark of a small mind"
(So did Sagacity explain the fault)
"As when it needs must square away and sink
To its own small dimensions, private scale
Of right and wrong,—humanity i' the large,
The right and wrong of the universe, forsooth!
This man addressed himself to guard and guide
Hohenstiel-Schwangau. When the case demands
He frustrate villany in the egg, unhatched,
With easy stamp and minimum of pang
E'en to the punished reptile, 'There 's my oath
Restrains my foot,' objects our guide and guard,
'I must leave guardianship and guidance now:
Rather than stretch one handbreadth of the law,
I am bound to see it break from end to end.
First show me death i' the body politic:
Then prescribe pill and potion, what may please
Hohenstiel-Schwangau! all is for her sake:
'T was she ordained my service should be so.
What if the event demonstrate her unwise,
If she unwill the thing she willed before?
I hold to the letter and obey the bond
And leave her to perdition loyally.'
Whence followed thrice the expenditure we blame
Of human life and liberty: for want
O' the by-blow, came deliberate butcher's-work!"

"Elsewhere go carry your complaint!" bade he.
"Least, largest, there 's one law for all the minds,
Here or above: be true at any price!
'T is just o' the great scale, that such happy stroke
Of falsehood would be found a failure. Truth
Still stands unshaken at her base by me,
Reigns paramount i' the world, for the large good

O' the long late generations,—I and you
Forgotten like this buried foolishness!
Not so the good I rooted in its grave."

This is why he refused to break his oath,
Rather appealed to the people, gained the power
To act as he thought best, then used it, once
For all, no matter what the consequence
To knaves and fools. As thus began his sway,
So, through its twenty years, one rule of right
Sufficed him: govern for the many first,
The poor mean multitude, all mouths and eyes:
Bid the few, better favored in the brain,
Be patient, nor presume on privilege,
Help him or else be quiet,—never crave
That he help them,—increase, forsooth, the gulf
Yawning so terribly 'twixt mind and mind
I' the world here, which his purpose was to block
At bottom, were it by an inch, and bridge,
If by a filament, no more, at top.
Equalize things a little! And the way
He took to work that purpose out, was plain
Enough to intellect and honesty
And—superstition, style it if you please,
So long as you allow there was no lack
O' the quality imperative in man—
Reverence. You see deeper? thus saw he,
And by the light he saw, must walk: how else
Was he to do his part? a man's, with might
And main, and not a faintest touch of fear,
Sure he was in the hand of God who comes
Before and after, with a work to do
Which no man helps nor hinders. Thus the man,—
So timid when the business was to touch
The uncertain order of humanity,
Imperil, for a problematic cure
Of grievance on the surface, any good
I' the deep of things, dim yet discernible,—
This same man, so irresolute before,
Show him a true excrescence to cut sheer,
A devil's graft on God's foundation-stock,
Then—no complaint of indecision more!
He wrenched out the whole canker, root and branch,
Deaf to who cried that earth would tumble in
At its four corners if he touched a twig.
Witness that lie of lies, arch-infamy,
When the Republic, with her life involved
In just this law—"Each people rules itself

Its own way, not as any stranger please"—
Turned, and for first proof she was living, bade
Hohenstiel-Schwangau fasten on the throat
Of the first neighbor that claimed benefit
O' the law herself established: "Hohenstiel
For Hohenstielers! Rome, by parity
Of reasoning, for Romans? That 's a jest
Wants proper treatment,—lancet—puncture suits
The proud flesh: Rome ape Hohenstiel forsooth!"
And so the siege and slaughter and success
Whereof we nothing doubt that Hohenstiel
Will have to pay the price, in God's good time.
Which does not always fall on Saturday
When the world looks for wages. Anyhow,
He found this infamy triumphant. Well:
Sagacity suggested, make this speech!
"The work was none of mine: suppose wrong wait,
Stand over for redressing? Mine for me,
My predecessors' work on their own head!
Meantime, there 's plain advantage, should we leave
Things as we find them. Keep Rome manacled
Hand and foot: no fear of unruliness!
Her foes consent to even seem our friends
So long, no longer. Then, there 's glory got
By boldness and bravado to the world:
The disconcerted world must grin and bear
The old saucy writing,—'Grunt thereat who may,
So shall things be, for such my pleasure is—
Hohenstiel-Schwangau's.' How that reads in Rome,
I' the capitol where Brennus broke his pate,
And lends a flourish to our journalists!"
Only, it was nor read nor flourished of,
Since, not a moment did such glory stay
Excision of the canker! Out it came,
Root and branch, with much roaring, and some blood,
And plentiful abuse of him from friend
And foe. Who cared? Not Nature, who assuaged
The pain and set the patient on his legs
Promptly: the better! had it been the worse,
'T is Nature you must try conclusions with,
Not he, since nursing canker kills the sick
For certain, while to cut may cure, at least.
"Ah," groaned a second time Sagacity,
"Again the little mind, precipitate,
Rash, rude, when even in the right, as here!
The great mind knows the power of gentleness,
Only tries force because persuasion fails.
Had this man, by prelusive trumpet-blast,

Signified, 'Truth and Justice mean to come,
Nay, fast approach your threshold! Ere they knock,
See that the house be set in order, swept
And garnished, windows shut, and doors thrown wide!
The free State comes to visit the free Church:
Receive her! or ... or ... never mind what else!'
Thus moral suasion heralding brute force,
How had he seen the old abuses die,
And new life kindle here, there, everywhere,
Roused simply by that mild yet potent spell—
Beyond or beat of drum or stroke of sword—
Public opinion!"

"How, indeed?" he asked,
"When all to see, after some twenty years,
Were your own fool-face waiting for the sight,
Faced by as wide a grin from ear to ear
O' the knaves who, while the fools were waiting, worked—
Broke yet another generation's heart—
Twenty years' respite helping! Teach your nurse
'Compliance with, before you suck, the teat!'
Find what that means, and meanwhile hold your tongue!"

Whereof the war came which he knew must be.

Now, this had proved the dry-rot of the race
He ruled o'er, that, i' the old day, when was need
They fought for their own liberty and life,
Well did they fight, none better: whence, such love
Of fighting somehow still for fighting's sake
Against no matter whose the liberty
And life, so long as self-conceit should crow
And clap the wing, while justice sheathed her claw,—
That what had been the glory of the world
When thereby came the world's good, grew its plague
Now that the champion-armor, donned to dare
The dragon once, was clattered up and down
Highway and by-path of the world, at peace,
Merely to mask marauding, or for sake
O' the shine and rattle that apprised the fields
Hohenstiel-Schwangau was a fighter yet,
And would be, till the weary world suppressed
Her peccant humors out of fashion now.
Accordingly the world spoke plain at last,
Promised to punish who next played with fire.

So, at his advent, such discomfiture
Taking its true shape of beneficence,

Hohenstiel-Schwangau, half-sad and part-wise,
Sat: if with wistful eye reverting oft
To each pet weapon, rusty on its peg,
Yet, with a sigh of satisfaction too
That, peacefulness become the law, herself
Got the due share of godsends in its train,
Cried shame and took advantage quietly.
Still, so the dry-rot had been nursed into
Blood, bones and marrow, that, from worst to best,
All,—clearest brains and soundest hearts save here,—
All had this lie acceptable for law
Plain as the sun at noonday—"War is best,
Peace is worst; peace we only tolerate
As needful preparation for new war:
War may be for whatever end we will—
Peace only as the proper help thereto.
Such is the law of right and wrong for us
Hohenstiel-Schwangau: for the other world,
As naturally, quite another law.
Are we content? The world is satisfied.
Discontent? Then the world must give us leave
To strike right, left, and exercise our arm
Torpid of late through overmuch repose,
And show its strength is still superlative
At somebody's expense in life or limb:
Which done,—let peace succeed and last a year!"
Such devil's-doctrine so was judged God's law,
We say, when this man stepped upon the stage,
That it had seemed a venial fault at most
Had he once more obeyed Sagacity.
"You come i' the happy interval of peace,
The favorable weariness from war:
Prolong it! artfully, as if intent
On ending peace as soon as possible.
Quietly so increase the sweets of ease
And safety, so employ the multitude,
Put hod and trowel so in idle hands,
So stuff and stop up wagging jaws with bread,
That selfishness shall surreptitiously
Do wisdom's office, whisper in the ear
Of Hohenstiel-Schwangau, there 's a pleasant feel
In being gently forced down, pinioned fast
To the easy arm-chair by the pleading arms
O' the world beseeching her to there abide
Content with all the harm done hitherto,
And let herself be petted in return,
Free to re-wage, in speech and prose and verse,
The old unjust wars, nay—in verse and prose

And speech,—to vaunt new victories, shall prove
A plague o' the future,—so that words suffice
For present comfort, and no deeds denote
That—tired of illimitable line on line
Of boulevard-building, tired o' the theatre
With the tuneful thousand in their thrones above,
For glory of the male intelligence,
And Nakedness in her due niche below,
For illustration of the female use—
That she, 'twixt yawn and sigh, prepares to slip
Out of the arm-chair, wants fresh blood again
From over the boundary, to color-up
The sheeny sameness, keep the world aware
Hohenstiel-Schwangau's arm needs exercise
Despite the petting of the universe!
Come, you 're a city-builder: what 's the way
Wisdom takes when time needs that she entice
Some fierce tribe, castled on the mountain-peak,
Into the quiet and amenity
O' the meadow-land below? By crying 'Done
With fight now, down with fortress'? Rather—'Dare
On, dare ever, not a stone displaced!'
Cries Wisdom: 'Cradle of our ancestors,
Be bulwark, give our children safety still!
Who of our children please may stoop and taste
O' the valley-fatness, unafraid,—for why?
At first alarm they have thy mother-ribs
To run upon for refuge; foes forget
Scarcely that Terror on her vantage-coign,
Couchant supreme among the powers of air,
Watches—prepared to pounce—the country wide!
Meanwhile the encouraged valley holds its own,
From the first hut's adventure in descent,
Half home, half hiding-place,—to dome and spire
Befitting the assured metropolis:
Nor means offence to the fort which caps the crag,
All undismantled of a turret-stone,
And bears the banner-pole that creaks at times
Embarrassed by the old emblazonment,
When festal days are to commemorate:
Otherwise left untenanted, no doubt,
Since, never fear, our myriads from below
Would rush, if needs were, man the walls again,
Renew the exploits of the earlier time
At moment's notice! But till notice sound,
Inhabit we in ease and opulence!'
And so, till one day thus a notice sounds,
Not trumpeted, but in a whisper-gust

Fitfully playing through mute city streets
At midnight weary of day's feast and game—
'Friends, your famed fort 's a ruin past repair!
Its use is—to proclaim it had a use
Obsolete long since. Climb and study there
How to paint barbican and battlement
I' the scenes of our new theatre! We fight
Now—by forbidding neighbors to sell steel
Or buy wine, not by blowing out their brains!
Moreover, while we let time sap the strength
O' the walls omnipotent in menace once,
Neighbors would seem to have prepared surprise—
Run up defences in a mushroom-growth,
For all the world like what we boasted: brief—
Hohenstiel-Schwangau's policy is peace!'"

Ay, so Sagacity advised him filch
Folly from fools; handsomely substitute
The dagger o' lath, while gay they sang and danced,
For that long dangerous sword they liked to feel,
Even at feast-time, clink and make friends start.
No! he said: "Hear the truth, and bear the truth,
And bring the truth to bear on all you are
And do, assured that only good comes thence
Whate'er the shape good take! While I have rule,
Understand!—war for war's sake, war for sake
O' the good war gets you as war's sole excuse,
Is damnable and damned shall be. You want
Glory? Why so do I, and so does God.
Where is it found,—in this paraded shame,—
One particle of glory? Once you warred
For liberty against the world, and won:
There was the glory. Now, you fain would war
Because the neighbor prospers overmuch,—
Because there has been silence half-an-hour,
Like Heaven on earth, without a cannon-shot
Announcing Hohenstielers-Schwangauese
Are minded to disturb the jubilee,—
Because the loud tradition echoes faint,
And who knows but posterity may doubt
If the great deeds were ever done at all,
Much less believe, were such to do again,
So the event would follow: therefore, prove
The old power, at the expense of somebody!
Oh, Glory,—gilded bubble, bard and sage
So nickname rightly,—would thy dance endure
One moment, would thy vaunting make believe
Only one eye thy ball was solid gold,

Hadst thou less breath to buoy thy vacancy
Than a whole multitude expends in praise,
Less range for roaming than from head to head
Of a whole people? Flit, fall, fly again,
Only, fix never where the resolute hand
May prick thee, prove the glassy lie thou art!
Give me real intellect to reason with,
No multitude, no entity that apes
One wise man, being but a million fools!
How and whence wishest glory, thou wise one?
Wouldst get it,—didst thyself guide Providence,—
By stinting of his due each neighbor round
In strength and knowledge and dexterity
So as to have thy littleness grow large
By all those somethings once, turned nothings now,
As children make a molehill mountainous
By scooping out a trench around their pile,
And saving so the mudwork from approach?
Quite otherwise the cheery game of life,
True yet mimetic warfare, whereby man
Does his best with his utmost, and so ends
The victor most of all in fair defeat.
Who thinks,—would he have no one think beside?
Who knows, who does,—save his must learning die
And action cease? Why, so our giant proves
No better than a dwarf, once rivalry
Prostrate around him. Let the whole race stand
For him to try conclusions fairly with!
Show me the great man would engage his peer
Rather by grinning 'Cheat, thy gold is brass!'
Than granting 'Perfect piece of purest ore!
Still, is it less good mintage, this of mine?'
Well, and these right and sound results of soul
I' the strong and healthy one wise man,—shall such
Be vainly sought for, scornfully renounced
I' the multitude that make the entity—
The people?—to what purpose, if no less,
In power and purity of soul, below
The reach of the unit than, by multiplied
Might of the body, vulgarized the more,
Above, in thick and threefold brutishness?
See! you accept such one wise man, myself:
Wiser or less wise, still I operate
From my own stock of wisdom, nor exact
Of other sort of natures you admire,
That whoso rhymes a sonnet pays a tax,
Who paints a landscape dips brush at his cost,
Who scores a septett true for strings and wind

Mulcted must be—else how should I impose
Properly, attitudinize aright,
Did such conflicting claims as these divert
Hohenstiel-Schwangau from observing me?
Therefore, what I find facile, you be sure,
With effort or without it, you shall dare—
You, I aspire to make my better self
And truly the Great Nation. No more war
For war's sake, then! and,—seeing, wickedness
Springs out of folly,—no more foolish dread
O' the neighbor waxing too inordinate
A rival, through his gain of wealth and ease!
What?—keep me patient, Powers!—the people here,
Earth presses to her heart, nor owns a pride
Above her pride i' the race all flame and air
And aspiration to the boundless Great,
The incommensurably Beautiful—
Whose very falterings groundward come of flight
Urged by a pinion all too passionate
For heaven and what it holds of gloom and glow:
Bravest of thinkers, bravest of the brave
Doers, exalt in Science, rapturous
In Art, the—more than all—magnetic race
To fascinate their fellows, mould mankind
Hohenstiel-Schwangau-fashion,—these, what?—these
Will have to abdicate their primacy
Should such a nation sell them steel untaxed,
And such another take itself, on hire
For the natural sennight, somebody for lord
Unpatronized by me whose back was turned?
Or such another yet would fain build bridge,
Lay rail, drive tunnel, busy its poor self
With its appropriate fancy: so there 's—flash—
Hohenstiel-Schwangau up in arms at once!
Genius has somewhat of the infantine:
But of the childish, not a touch nor taint
Except through self-will, which, being foolishness,
Is certain, soon or late, of punishment.
Which Providence avert!—and that it may
Avert what both of us would so deserve,
No foolish dread o' the neighbor, I enjoin!
By consequence, no wicked war with him,
While I rule!

"Does that mean—no war at all
When just the wickedness I here proscribe
Comes, haply, from the neighbor? Does my speech
Precede the praying that you beat the sword

To ploughshare, and the spear to pruning-hook,
And sit down henceforth under your own vine
And fig-tree through the sleepy summer month,
Letting what hurly-burly please explode
On the other side the mountain-frontier? No,
Beloved! I foresee and I announce
Necessity of warfare in one case,
For one cause: one way, I bid broach the blood
O' the world. For truth and right, and only right
And truth,—right, truth, on the absolute scale of God,
No pettiness of man's admeasurement,—
In such case only, and for such one cause,
Fight your hearts out, whatever fate betide
Hands energetic to the uttermost!
Lie not! Endure no lie which needs your heart
And hand to push it out of mankind's path—
No lie that lets the natural forces work
Too long ere lay it plain and pulverized—
Seeing man's life lasts only twenty years!
And such a lie, before both man and God,
Proving, at this time present, Austria's rule
O'er Italy,—for Austria's sake the first,
Italy's next, and our sake last of all,
Come with me and deliver Italy!
Smite hip and thigh until the oppressor leave
Free from the Adriatic to the Alps
The oppressed one! We were they who laid her low
In the old bad day when Villany braved Truth
And Right, and laughed 'Henceforward, God deposed,
Satan we set to rule forevermore
I' the world!'—whereof to stop the consequence,
And for atonement of false glory there
Gaped at and gabbled over by the world,
I purpose to get God enthroned again
For what the world will gird at as sheer shame
I' the cost of blood and treasure, 'All for naught—
Not even, say, some patch of province, splice
O' the frontier?—some snug honorarium-fee
Shut into glove and pocketed apace?'
(Questions Sagacity) 'in deference
To the natural susceptibility
Of folks at home, unwitting of that pitch
You soar to, and misdoubting if Truth, Right
And the other such augustnesses repay
Expenditure in coin o' the realm,—but prompt
To recognize the cession of Savoy
And Nice as marketable value!' No,
Sagacity, go preach to Metternich,

And, sermon ended, stay where he resides!
Hohenstiel-Schwangau, you and I must march
The other road! war for the hate of war,
Not love, this once!" So Italy was free.

What else noteworthy and commendable
I' the man's career?—that he was resolute—
No trepidation, much less treachery
On his part, should imperil from its poise
The ball o' the world, heaved up at such expense
Of pains so far, and ready to rebound,
Let but a finger maladroitly fall,
Under pretence of making fast and sure
The inch gained by late volubility,
And run itself back to the ancient rest
At foot o' the mountain. Thus he ruled, gave proof
The world had gained a point, progressive so,
By choice, this time, as will and power concurred,
O' the fittest man to rule; not chance of birth,
Or such-like dice-throw. Oft Sagacity
Was at his ear: "Confirm this clear advance,
Support this wise procedure! You, elect
O' the people, mean to justify their choice
And out-king all the kingly imbeciles;
But that 's just half the enterprise: remains
You find them a successor like yourself,
In head and heart and eye and hand and aim,
Or all done 's undone; and whom hope to mould
So like you as the pupil Nature sends,
The son and heir's completeness which you lack?
Lack it no longer! Wed the pick o' the world,
Where'er you think you find it. Should she be
A queen,—tell Hohenstielers-Schwangauese,
'So do the old enthroned decrepitudes
Acknowledge, in the rotten hearts of them,
Their knell is knolled, they hasten to make peace
With the new order, recognize in me
Your right to constitute what king you will,
Cringe therefore crown in hand and bride on arm,
To both of us: we triumph, I suppose!'
Is it the other sort of rank?—bright eye,
Soft smile, and so forth, all her queenly boast?
Undaunted the exordium—'I, the man
O' the people, with the people mate myself:
So stand, so fall. Kings, keep your crowns and brides!
Our progeny (if Providence agree)
Shall live to tread the baubles underfoot
And bid the scarecrows consort with their kin.

For son, as for his sire, be the free wife
In the free state!'"

That is, Sagacity
Would prop up one more lie, the most of all
Pernicious fancy that the son and heir
Receives the genius from the sire, himself
Transmits as surely,—ask experience else!
Which answers,—never was so plain a truth
As that God drops his seed of heavenly flame
Just where he wills on earth: sometimes where man
Seems to tempt—such the accumulated store
Of faculties—one spark to fire the heap;
Sometimes where, fireball-like, it falls upon
The naked unpreparèdness of rock,
Burns, beaconing the nations through their night.
Faculties, fuel for the flame? All helps
Come, ought to come, or come not, crossed by chance,
From culture and transmission. What 's your want
I' the son and heir? Sympathy, aptitude,
Teachableness, the fuel for the flame?
You 'll have them for your pains: but the flame's self,
The novel thought of God shall light the world?
No, poet, though your offspring rhyme and chime
I' the cradle,—painter, no, for all your pet
Draws his first eye, beats Salvatore's boy,—And
thrice no, statesman, should your progeny
Tie bib and tucker with no tape but red,
And make a foolscap-kite of protocols!
Critic and copyist and bureaucrat
To heart's content! The seed o' the apple-tree
Brings forth another tree which bears a crab:
'T is the great gardener grafts the excellence
On wildings where he will.

"How plain I view,
Across those misty years 'twixt me and Rome"—
(Such the man's answer to Sagacity)
"The little wayside temple, halfway down
To a mild river that makes oxen white
Miraculously, un-mouse-colors skin,
Or so the Roman country people dream!
I view that sweet small shrub-embedded shrine
On the declivity, was sacred once
To a transmuting Genius of the land,
Could touch and turn its dunnest natures bright,
—Since Italy means the Land of the Ox, we know.
Well, how was it the due succession fell

From priest to priest who ministered i' the cool
Calm fane o' the Clitumnian god? The sire
Brought forth a son and sacerdotal sprout,
Endowed instinctively with good and grace
To suit the gliding gentleness below—
Did he? Tradition tells another tale.
Each priest obtained his predecessor's staff,
Robe, fillet and insignia, blamelessly,
By springing out of ambush, soon or late,
And slaying him: the initiative rite
Simply was murder, save that murder took,
I' the case, another and religious name.
So it was once, is now, shall ever be
With genius and its priesthood in this world:
The new power slays the old—but handsomely.
There he lies, not diminished by an inch
Of stature that he graced the altar with,
Though somebody of other bulk and build
Cries, 'What a goodly personage lies here
Reddening the water where the bulrush roots!
May I conduct the service in his place,
Decently and in order, as did he,
And, as he did not, keep a wary watch
When meditating 'neath yon willow shade!'
Find out your best man, sure the son of him
Will prove best man again, and, better still
Somehow than best, the grandson-prodigy!
You think the world would last another day
Did we so make us masters of the trick
Whereby the works go, we could pre-arrange
Their play and reach perfection when we please?
Depend on it, the change and the surprise
Are part o' the plan: 't is we wish steadiness;
Nature prefers a motion by unrest,
Advancement through this force which jostles that.
And so, since much remains i' the world to see,
Here 's the world still, affording God the sight."
Thus did the man refute Sagacity,
Ever at this old whisper in his ear:
"Here are you picked out, by a miracle,
And placed conspicuously enough, folks say
And you believe, by Providence outright
Taking a new way—nor without success—
To put the world upon its mettle: good!
But Fortune alternates with Providence;
Resource is soon exhausted. Never count
On such a happy hit occurring twice!
Try the old method next time!"

"Old enough,"
(At whisper in his ear, the laugh outbroke,)
"And mode the most discredited of all,
By just the men and women who make boast
They are kings and queens thereby! Mere self-defence
Should teach them, on one chapter of the law
Must be no sort of trifling—chastity:
They stand or fall, as their progenitors
Were chaste or unchaste. Now, run eye around
My crowned acquaintance, give each life its look
And no more,—why, you 'd think each life was led
Purposely for example of what pains
Who leads it took to cure the prejudice,
And prove there 's nothing so unprovable
As who is who, what son of what a sire,
And—inferentially—how faint the chance
That the next generation needs to fear
Another fool o' the selfsame type as he
Happily regnant now by right divine
And luck o' the pillow! No: select your lord
By the direct employment of your brains
As best you may,—bad as the blunder prove,
A far worse evil stank beneath the sun
When some legitimate blockhead managed so
Matters that high time was to interfere,
Though interference came from hell itself
And not the blind mad miserable mob
Happily ruled so long by pillow-luck
And divine right,—by lies in short, not truth.
And meanwhile use the allotted minute ..."

One,—
Two, three, four, five—yes, five the pendule warns!
Eh? Why, this wild work wanders past all bound
And bearing! Exile, Leicester Square, the life
I' the old gay miserable time, rehearsed,
Tried on again like cast clothes, still to serve
At a pinch, perhaps? "Who 's who?" was aptly asked,
Since certainly I am not I! since when?
Where is the bud-mouthed arbitress? A nod
Out-Homering Homer! Stay—there flits the clue
I fain would find the end of! Yes,—"Meanwhile,
Use the allotted minute!" Well, you see,
(Veracious and imaginary Thiers,
Who map out thus the life I might have led,
But did not,—all the worse for earth and me,—
Doff spectacles, wipe pen, shut book, decamp!)

You see 't is easy in heroics! Plain
Pedestrian speech shall help me perorate.
Ah, if one had no need to use the tongue!
How obvious and how easy 't is to talk
Inside the soul, a ghostly dialogue—
Instincts with guesses,—instinct, guess, again
With dubious knowledge, half-experience: each
And all the interlocutors alike
Subordinating,—as decorum bids,
Oh, never fear! but still decisively,—
Claims from without that take too high a tone,
—("God wills this, man wants that, the dignity
Prescribed a prince would wish the other thing")—
Putting them back to insignificance
Beside one intimatest fact—myself
Am first to be considered, since I live
Twenty years longer and then end, perhaps!
But, where one ceases to soliloquize,
Somehow the motives, that did well enough
I' the darkness, when you bring them into light
Are found, like those famed cave-fish, to lack eye
And organ for the upper magnitudes.
The other common creatures, of less fine
Existence, that acknowledge earth and heaven,
Have it their own way in the argument.
Yes, forced to speak, one stoops to say—one's aim
Was—what it peradventure should have been:
To renovate a people, mend or end
That bane come of a blessing meant the world—
Inordinate culture of the sense made quick
By soul,—the lust o' the flesh, lust of the eye,
And pride of life,—and, consequent on these,
The worship of that prince o' the power o' the air
Who paints the cloud and fills the emptiness
And bids his votaries, famishing for truth,
Feed on a lie.

Alack, one lies one's self
Even in the stating that one's end was truth,
Truth only, if one states as much in words!
Give me the inner chamber of the soul
For obvious easy argument! 't is there
One pits the silent truth against a lie—
Truth which breaks shell a careless simple bird,
Nor wants a gorget nor a beak filed fine,
Steel spurs and the whole armory o' the tongue,
To equalize the odds. But, do your best,
Words have to come: and somehow words deflect

As the best cannon ever rifled will.

"Deflect" indeed! nor merely words from thoughts
But names from facts: "Clitumnus" did I say?
As if it had been his ox-whitening wave
Whereby folk practised that grim cult of old—
The murder of their temple's priest by who
Would qualify for his succession. Sure—
Nemi was the true lake's style. Dream had need
Of the ox-whitening peace of prettiness
And so confused names, well known once awake.

So, i' the Residenz yet, not Leicester Square,
Alone,—no such congenial intercourse!—
My reverie concludes, as dreaming should,
With daybreak: nothing done and over yet,
Except cigars! The adventure thus may be,
Or never needs to be at all: who knows?
My Cousin-Duke, perhaps, at whose hard head
—Is it, now—is this letter to be launched,
The sight of whose gray oblong, whose grim seal,
Set all these fancies floating for an hour?

Twenty years are good gain, come what come will!
Double or quits! The letter goes! Or stays?

Robert Browning – A Short Biography

He is the equal of any Victorian Poet that could be mentioned. However, Browning continues to be in the shadow of Tennyson, Arnold, Hopkins, Morris and many others.

Robert Browning was born on May 7th, 1812 in Walworth in the parish of Camberwell, London. He was baptized on June 14th, 1812, at Lock's Fields Independent Chapel, York Street, Walworth.

Browning's early years were certainly very interesting. His mother was an excellent pianist and a very devout evangelical Christian. His father, who worked as a clerk at the Bank of England, was also an artist, scholar, antiquarian, and collector of books and pictures. Indeed, he amassed more than 6,000 volumes of rare books including works in Greek, Hebrew, Latin, French, Italian, and Spanish. For the young and curious Browning, it was a wonderful resource, added to which his father was a guiding force in his education.

Many accounts attest that Browning was already proficient at reading and writing by the age of five. He is said to have been a bright but anxious student and to have studied and learnt Latin, Greek, and French by the time he was fourteen. From fourteen to sixteen he was educated at home, tutored in music, drawing, dancing, and horsemanship. Certainly, language and the arts were two areas the young Browning both absorbed and pushed himself towards.

At the age of twelve he wrote a volume of Byronic verse he called Incondita, which his parents attempted to have published. The attempts were unsuccessful and, disappointed, Browning destroyed the work.

In 1825, a cousin gave Browning a collection of Percy Bysshe Shelley's poetry; Browning was so enamored with the poems that he asked for the rest of Shelley's works for his thirteenth birthday. In fact, Browning then went the extra mile, declaring himself to be both a vegetarian and an atheist in honour of his hero.

Intriguingly it seems that the rejection of his first volume didn't dim his appreciation of other poets, but it appears to have stopped him writing any poems between the ages of thirteen and twenty.

In 1828, Browning enrolled at the newly-opened University of London. He was uncomfortable with the experience and he soon left, anxious to read and absorb at his own pace.

His education which, overall is notably rambling and lacks a structure that many of his artistic contemporaries enjoyed, i.e. excellent public schooling and then a degree at Oxford or Cambridge, may present many of his critics with ammunition to criticize, but alternatively his hap-hazard education certainly contributed to many of the references that baffled both critics and his audience, but they tellingly show the breath and scale of what he could turn words too. What others would call obscure references were, to Browning, remarkably obvious.

Browning's early career was very promising. His long poem Pauline (of which only a fragment was ever finished and published) brought him to the attention of the Pre-Raphaelite master Dante Gabriel Rossetti and his difficult Paracelsus (published in 1835) was warmly admired by both Dickens and Wordsworth.

In the 1830s he met the actor William Macready and was encouraged to develop and turn his talents to the stage by writing verse drama. But these plays, including Strafford, which ran for five nights in 1837, and those contained within the Bells and Pomegranates series, were, for the most part, unsuccessful.

During this period Browning began to discover that his real talents lay in taking a single character and allowing that character to discover more about himself by revealing further personal aspects of himself in his speeches; the dramatic monologue. The techniques he developed through this—especially the use of diction, rhythm, and symbol—are regarded as his most important contribution to poetry. They would later influence such major poets of the 20th Century as Ezra Pound, T. S. Eliot, and Robert Frost.

By 1840, with the publication of Sordello, the tide turned somewhat. Many thought he was being deliberately obscure, opaque beyond measure and his poetry for the next decade or so was not eagerly acquired or talked about.

As Browning attempted to rehabilitate his career he began a relationship with Elizabeth Barrett in 1845. He had read her poems and, being totally charmed by their quality, was determined to meet her. The poetess was better known than the younger Browning but suffered from a debilitating illness and was also subject to the harsh behaviour of her over-bearing father. Nevertheless, the new couple were soon inseparable.

Her father, as he did with any of his children that married, disinherited her. Despite this she had some money from her own resources and sensing that the best outcome for both the relationship and her own health was to move abroad the couple did just that. After a private marriage at St Marylebone Parish Church, in September 1846, they journeyed to Europe to honeymoon in Paris.

Their new life now took them to Italy, first to Pisa and a little later to Florence. There they absorbed life and one another.

But in the short term the literary assault on Browning's work did not let up. He was now criticized by such patrician writers as Charles Kingsley for his abandonment of England for foreign lands. Browning could do little to answer these attacks except to compose with his pen and continue with his poetical journey.

The Browning's were well respected, and even famous. Elizabeth health began to improve, she grew stronger and in 1849, at the age of 43, between four miscarriages, she gave birth to a son, Robert Wiedeman Barrett Browning, whom they nicknamed "Penini" or "Pen",

Intriguingly despite his growing reputation and return to form as a poet he was more often than not known as 'Elizabeth Barrett's husband'.

Work flowed from his pen that was to ensure his reputation as one of England's leading poets. When his collection Men and Women was published in 1855 it contained some of his finest lines. It was dedicated to Elizabeth. Life had begun to smile handsome rewards upon the Brownings.

Victorian society was very much taken with all things spiritualist. It was not enough to have command of much of the globe through Empire, they wished to know and explore wherever they could. The spirit world beckoned their interest. Browning dissented from this view believing it was all a hoax and a fraud. Elizabeth, however, was inclined to believe and this caused several disagreements between the couple.

They attended a séance by Daniel Dunglas Home, in July 1855. (Home was a famous and clamored after Scottish physical medium with the reported ability to levitate and speak with the dead). It is said that during this séance a spirit face materialised. Home then claimed it was the face of Browning's son who had died in infancy. Browning seized the 'materialisation' which turned out to be Home's bare foot. Browning had never lost a son in infancy.

After the séance, Browning wrote an angry letter to The Times, in which he said: "the whole display of hands, spirit utterances etc., was a cheat and imposture."

The Browning's time in Italy were immensely rewarding years for both their personal and professional lives. Browning encouraged her to include Sonnets from the Portuguese in her published works, these beautiful poems are undoubtedly one of the highlights of English love poetry.

Elizabeth had become quite politicised during these years. Engrossed in Italian politics (which was continuing to slowly re-unify the country), she issued a small volume of political poems entitled Poems before Congress (1860) most of which were written to express her sympathy with the Italian cause after the earlier outbreak of The Second Italian Independence War in 1859. In England they caused uproar. Conservative magazines such as Blackwood's and the Saturday Review labelled her a fanatic. She dedicated the book to her husband.

But in 1861 tragedy struck.

The couple had spent the winter of 1860–61 in Rome when Elizabeth's health deteriorated again and they returned to Florence in early June. However, these turned out to be her final weeks. Only morphine would now still the pain. She died in Browning's arms on June 29th, 1861. Browning said that she died "smilingly, happily, and with a face like a girl's .... Her last word was .... "Beautiful".

Her burial took place in the nearby Protestant English Cemetery of Florence. The local people were deeply saddened, and shops closed their doors in grief and respect.

Browning and their son were obviously devastated. Unable to bear being in Florence without Elizabeth they soon returned to London to live at 19 Warwick Crescent, Maida Vale.

As he re-integrated himself back into the London literary scene he began to finally receive the proper praise, respect and reputation that his works deserved.

Browning went on to publish Dramatis Personæ (1864), and The Ring and the Book (1868–1869). The latter, based on an "old yellow book" which told of a seventeenth-century Italian murder trial, received wide and generous critical acclaim. Although by now he was in the twilight of a long and prolific career, that had achieved some notable ups and downs, he was respected and indeed renowned for his talents and works.

In 1878, he revisited Italy for the first time since Elizabeth's death. He would return there on several further occasions but never to Florence.

Such was the esteem he was held in that The Browning Society was founded in 1881. Although he had never obtained a degree (something that set him apart from many other Victorian poets) he was now awarded honorary degrees from Oxford University in 1882 and then the University of Edinburgh in 1884.

In 1887, Browning produced the major work of his later years, Parleyings with Certain People of Importance in Their Day. Browning now spoke with his own voice as he engaged in a series of dialogues with long-forgotten figures of literary, artistic, and philosophic history. Unfortunately, both the critics and public were completely baffled by this.

On April 7th, 1889 Browning attended a dinner party at the home of his friend, the artist Rudolf Lehmann. The highlight of which was a recording made on a wax cylinder on an Edison cylinder phonograph. On the recording, which still exists, Browning recites part of How They Brought the Good News from Ghent to Aix, and can even be heard apologising when he forgets the words.

The recording was first played in 1890 on the anniversary of his death, at a gathering of his admirers, it was said to be the first time anyone's voice 'had been heard from beyond the grave'.

His last work Asolando: Fancies and Facts (1889), returned to his brief and concise lyric verse that was so popular. It was published on the day of his death on December 12th, 1889, Robert Browning was at his son's home Ca' Rezzonico in Venice.

He was buried in Poets' Corner in Westminster Abbey; his grave lies immediately adjacent to that of Alfred Tennyson.

Among the many who have publicly acknowledged their literary debt to him are Henry James, Oscar Wilde, George Bernard Shaw, G. K. Chesterton, Ezra Pound, Jorge Luis Borges, and Vladimir Nabokov.

Robert Browning - A Concise Bibliography

Here follows a list of the plays and poetry volumes published during his lifetime. Poems of particular worth are noted from within those volumes.

Pauline: A Fragment of a Confession (1833)
Paracelsus (1835)
Strafford (play) (1837)
Sordello (1840)
Bells and Pomegranates No. I: Pippa Passes (play) (1841)
 The Year's at the Spring
Bells and Pomegranates No. II: King Victor and King Charles (play) (1842)
Bells and Pomegranates No. III: Dramatic Lyrics (1842)
 Porphyria's Lover
 Soliloquy of the Spanish Cloister
 My Last Duchess
 The Pied Piper of Hamelin
 Count Gismond
 Johannes Agricola in Meditation
Bells and Pomegranates No. IV: The Return of the Druses (play) (1843)
Bells and Pomegranates No. V: A Blot in the 'Scutcheon (play) (1843)
Bells and Pomegranates No. VI: Colombe's Birthday (play) (1844)
Bells and Pomegranates No. VII: Dramatic Romances and Lyrics (1845)
 The Laboratory
 How They Brought the Good News from Ghent to Aix
 The Bishop Orders His Tomb at Saint Praxed's Church
 The Lost Leader
 Home Thoughts from Abroad
 Meeting at Night
Bells and Pomegranates No. VIII: Luria and A Soul's Tragedy (plays) (1846)
Christmas-Eve and Easter-Day (1850)
An Essay on Percy Bysshe Shelley (essay) (1852)
Two Poems (1854)
Men and Women (1855)
 Love Among the Ruins
 A Toccata of Galuppi's
 Childe Roland to the Dark Tower Came
 Fra Lippo Lippi
 Andrea Del Sarto
 The Patriot

The Last Ride Together
Memorabilia
Cleon
How It Strikes a Contemporary
The Statue and the Bust
A Grammarian's Funeral
An Epistle Containing the Strange Medical Experience of Karshish, the Arab Physician
Bishop Blougram's Apology
Master Hugues of Saxe-Gotha
By the Fire-side

Dramatis Personae (1864)

Caliban upon Setebos
Rabbi Ben Ezra
Abt Vogler
Mr. Sludge, "The Medium"
Prospice
A Death in the Desert

The Ring and the Book (1868–69)
Balaustion's Adventure (1871)
Prince Hohenstiel-Schwangau, Saviour of Society (1871)
Fifine at the Fair (1872)
Red Cotton Night-Cap Country, or, Turf and Towers (1873)
Aristophanes' Apology (1875)

Thamuris Marching

The Inn Album (1875)
Pacchiarotto, and How He Worked in Distemper (1876)

Numpholeptos

The Agamemnon of Aeschylus (1877)
La Saisiaz and The Two Poets of Croisic (1878)
Dramatic Idylls (1879)
Dramatic Idylls: Second Series (1880)

Pan and Luna

Jocoseria (1883)
Ferishtah's Fancies (1884)
Parleyings with Certain People of Importance in Their Day (1887)
Asolando (1889)

Prologue
Summum Bonum
Bad Dreams III
Flute-Music, with an Accompaniment
Epilogue

www.ingramcontent.com/pod-product-compliance
Lightning Source LLC
LaVergne TN
LVHW010546100826
845148LV00013B/2626